Learning through Talk

Learning through Talk is a practical handbook. It is designed to help teachers and others working with 5 to 11 year olds develop the key skills, which will enable their pupils to use talk effectively for learning. The activities within the book encourage thinking and learning across the curriculum and help pupils to improve their communication skills and become independent learners.

This book provides:

- advice and practical guidance on developing the essential skills of participation, collaboration, building on, positive challenge, resolving differences and reflection;
- a series of motivating and exciting workshop activities;
- photocopiable resources to support workshops with links to video material on the companion website.

A practical, blended resource, *Learning through Talk* helps teachers shift their focus to evaluate the quality of pupils' talk as an insight into the learning process. The authors present tried-and-tested methods for reflection, including the use of a video diary room, an example of which is accessible online via the companion website.

An invaluable guide for both trainee and practising teachers, this book will provide those working with children with a practical framework to improve talk and communication in their classrooms in line with recent curriculum developments.

Heather Luxford is an Advanced Skills Teacher for Creativity and Thinking Skills, Teaching and Learning and Gifted and Talented Pupils and a Key Stage 2 classroom teacher at two rural schools in West Sussex.

Lizzie Smart is a Teacher Trainer, based at the University of Chichester where she teaches English to student teachers in training and to practising professionals on the Masters courses. She also inspects initial teacher training for Ofsted.

Learning through Talk

Developing Learning Dialogues in the Primary Classroom

Heather Luxford and Lizzie Smart

Routledge
Taylor & Francis Group

LONDON AND NEW YORK

First published 2009
by Routledge
2 Park Square, Milton Park, Abingdon, Oxon OX14 4RN

Simultaneously published in the USA and Canada
by Routledge
270 Madison Avenue, New York, NY 10016

Routledge is an imprint of the Taylor & Francis Group, an informa business

© 2009 Heather Luxford and Lizzie Smart

Typeset in Bembo and Bliss by
Florence Production Ltd, Stoodleigh, Devon
Printed and bound in Great Britain by
MPG Books Group, UK

British Library Cataloguing in Publication Data
A catalogue record for this book is available from the British Library

Library of Congress Cataloging-in-Publication Data
Luxford, Heather.
  Learning through talk: developing learning dialogues in the primary
  classroom/Heather Luxford and Lizzie Smart.
      p. cm.
    Includes bibliographical references.
  1. Oral communication – Study and teaching (Elementary).
  2. Interpersonal communication – Study and teaching (Elementary).
  I. Smart, Lizzie.   II. Title.
  LB1572.L88 2009
    372.62—dc22   2008054239

ISBN10: 0–415–48521–5 (pbk)

ISBN13: 978–0–415–48521–0 (pbk)

Contents

Acknowledgements

The authors would like to thank the following for their contributions, help and support. First, to the staff, parents, and most importantly, to all the Year Four and Five pupils, past and present, from St Mary's Church of England First School, Washington and Thakeham First School, both in West Sussex. Second, to our families: Paul, Ian, Jamie and Michael, for both technical and moral support and help.

Abbreviations

The following common abbreviations are used in this book:

AfL   Assessment for Learning
DCSF   Department for Children, Schools and Families
DfEE   Department for Education and Employment
DfES   Department for Education and Skills
NC   National Curriculum
PSHE   Personal, social and health education
QCA   Qualifications and Curriculum Authority
TA   Teaching assistant

Illustrations

Figures

Photos

Tables

Resources

Introduction

Why learning through talk matters

On discovering that talk was to be the focus of a research project in her classroom, one child responded in astonishment, 'when I found out we were going to be learning talk, I thought whoa, you're teaching us how to talk and we know how to do that already!' Many children and teachers in primary classrooms may well feel the same way. It is undoubtedly true that much talking by children, teachers and others in the school community, goes on both inside and outside of classrooms. The majority of us use talk confidently as our principle method of communication.

However, that talk may not be (and should not always be) focused on learning. We are certainly not implying that this other, social and communicative talk should not happen – it is important for building the social cohesion on which good classrooms flourish. However, we strongly believe that the power of talk as a learning medium has not yet been harnessed fully, perhaps because developing this type of classroom talk takes time that busy teachers have been unable to spare. In a decade or so of educational change, practitioners have been so focused on delivering the primary curriculum and national strategies that developing children's talk for learning may not have been a priority, as they tried to assess whether learning objectives had been met and at what level.

It is also the case that the absence of any objectives directly relating to speaking and listening in *The National Literacy Strategy: Framework for Teaching* (DfEE, 1998) meant that for many years these skills were sidelined by some teachers in their desire, supported by the push from government, to raise standards in reading and writing. However, the curriculum objectives for speaking and listening are there in the newer *Primary Framework for Literacy and Mathematics* (DfES, 2006) and imply that children should be using dialogic talk. In Year Six one of the speaking objectives states that 'most children should learn to use the techniques of dialogic talk to explore ideas, topics and issues'. (p. 34).

However, there has been little guidance to date on how to build up the skills necessary to enable children to achieve this, or even clear explanation of what dialogic talk means. There is a brief description in the glossary of *Speaking, Listening, Learning: Working with Children in Key Stages 1 and 2*, where it states:

> Teaching through dialogue enables teachers and pupils to share and build on ideas in sustained talk. When teaching through dialogue, teachers encourage children to listen to each other, share ideas and consider alternatives; build on their own and other's ideas to develop coherent thinking; express their views fully and help each other to reach common understandings. Teaching through dialogue can take place when a teacher talks with an individual pupil, or two pupils are talking together or when the whole class is joining in a discussion.
>
> (DfES, 2003b: 35)

This description is not supported by an explanation of the skills needed to achieve this type of talk.

We firmly agree with Robin Alexander (2006: 26) when he states that the best talk is, 'purposeful and productive dialogue where questions, answers and feedback build into coherent and expanding chains of enquiry'. It is this type of talk that has the power to develop learning and it is this type of talk that this book seeks to address and promote through the suggested teaching programme. This way of learning through talk is the start of the development of a lifelong skill that chimes well with the five stated outcomes of *Every Child Matters: Change for Children* (DfES, 2004b), particularly outcomes three and four: 'Enjoy and Achieve and Make a Positive Contribution'. Children's confidence in their own personal and social development and their ability to meet and negotiate challenges will be significantly increased by effective talk skills. Because *The Assessment for Learning Strategy* (DCSF, 2008) assumes that children and teachers can use talk for learning across the curriculum, it is important to develop the necessary skills to ensure this happens as the strategy rolls out over the next three years.

Who talks?

We know from our own research and that carried out by Hardman, Smith and Wall (2003), Alexander (2006) and others, that in classrooms the dominant speaker is often the teacher and children's independent talk is limited; yet classrooms often depend on teachers having time to work with focus groups while other groups learn without direct teacher support.

The aim of this book is to help teachers and others involved in classroom learning and teaching, such as teaching assistants (TAs) and trainee teachers, to develop children's talk for learning through a series of workshops, each of which is focused on developing a talk for learning related skill. The intended outcome is children who are confident in using talk to engage in collaborative work and develop their thinking and learning, with or without the presence of the teacher or another adult. Our experience tells us that this takes time and the quality of talk in some of the initial activities may be limited. Follow the activities through each stage, however, and it is possible to notice a difference. It is worth tracking this improvement to ensure the impetus to carry on is sustained in the knowledge that progress is being made. Following the programme will also help teachers to reflect on their own use of talk and therefore lead to changes in the quality of teacher-child exchanges.

As a starting point for developing talk, it is pertinent to video a short teaching and learning activity, involving both teacher and children, and to evaluate how talk is currently used in the classroom and who the dominant talkers and listeners are. The following simple, introductory questions might provide a good focus for evaluation:

- Who does most of the talking?

- What do you notice about the talk? What kind of talk is it?

- Do your children respond only to you or also to each other?

- What type of questions do you ask?

- What do you notice about both length and quality of children's responses?

Alexander's research (2006) showed that teacher values were much more important than teacher strategies in the move to a dialogic classroom: teachers had to want to develop their practice and understand the benefits it could bring. This simple evaluation of current practice can provide the impetus needed for change.

Why now?

Talk is fashionable again after its period in the shadows. The emphasis on high-quality talk underpinning the development of reading and writing is prevalent in the *Independent Review of the Teaching of Early Reading*, where Jim Rose notes the need to raise the profile of talk as it can, 'exert the greatest leverage on children's learning and understanding' (Rose, 2006: 17). Alongside and supporting this, the inclusion of the Speaking and Listening objectives in the *Primary Framework for Literacy and Mathematics* (DfES, 2006) and in the *Early Years Foundation Stage* (DfES, 2007), as well as *The Assessment for Learning Strategy* (DCSF, 2008), have ensured that schools and teachers will refocus attention on talk. It is also mentioned in the recently published interim report of the *Independent Primary Review* where Jim Rose notes:

> Discussion of reading, writing and numeracy in primary education sometimes fails to recognise the central importance of developing children's spoken communication. The primary skills of speaking and listening are essential in their own right and as a crucial platform for learning to read and write, to be numerate and, indeed, to be successful in virtually all of the learning children undertake at school and elsewhere.
>
> (Rose, 2008: 42, sect. 2, para. 2.41)

Its time has come.

However, research supporting the development of quality talk for learning has not kept pace with that supporting other aspects of the curriculum. Our research found it necessary to revisit the work carried out by the National Oracy Project during the last century, where it was noted that 'the central justification for talk in the classroom lies in its capacity to deepen and enhance the quality of children's learning' (Baddeley, 1992: 40). The professional development materials associated with the Speaking and Listening element of *The National Curriculum: Handbook for Primary Teachers in England* (DfEE/QCA, 1999) understandably focus on developing and measuring the skills noted in the objectives. The ideas developed in this book draw on the work of key researchers in the field of children's talk. We recommend teachers to seek out the work of Barnes and Todd (1977, 1995), Bakhtin (1981), Mercer (1995, 2000), Wergerif (1996), Fisher (2003, 2005) and Lambirth (2006), and in particular the work of Alexander (2003, 2004a, 2004b, 2006, 2007), details of which can be found in the Bibliography.

We feel strongly that busy teachers need practical support to develop a classroom where dialogic talk flourishes. Thus, this series of practical workshop activities was devised, implemented and evaluated. We know from our work with teachers at all stages of their professional development that this practical approach gives them the confidence they need to take the next step in developing a classroom where children and teachers learn through talk.

Terminology

We have deliberately decided to use the term 'talk' throughout this book. 'Speaking' and 'listening' have firm associations with the Programme of Study of the same name in the English section of *The National Curriculum* (DfEE/QCA, 1999) and in the *Primary Framework for Literacy and Mathematics* (DfES, 2006). Elements of the activities suggested in this book certainly support the objectives in this Programme of Study and their detailing in the *Primary Framework*. Indeed, we believe that children will be better equipped to address the objectives and reach a high standard of attainment if they have access to a teaching programme like this one. However, there are also clear links across the curriculum and we firmly believe that talk is best considered as a cross-curricular skill. One of the more obvious of these links is to the non-statutory guidelines for personal, social and health education and citizenship at Key Stages 1 and 2 in *The National Curriculum* (DfES/QCA, 1999), where developing children's role as good citizens is predicated on their being able to engage in dialogue with others. However, we also give examples linked to science, and the talk skills discussed in each chapter could be successfully deployed across most aspects the primary curriculum.

Some of the terms commonly used to describe speaking and listening in the curriculum documentation are not our preferred terms. The Programmes of Study for Speaking and Listening use the term 'discussion'. Our preferred term is 'dialogue'; one that *The Assessment for Learning Strategy* (DCSF, 2008) echoes strongly. A discussion implies a conversation or debate about a topic. There is no need to come to any agreement. In contrast, the term 'dialogue' or 'dialogic talk' is considered in the glossary for the handbook of the *Primary National Strategy for Speaking, Listening, Learning: Working with Children in Key Stages 1 and 2* (DfES, 2003b: 35) where it is described as enabling children to, 'reach common understandings'. It is these common understandings that help learning progress.

Effective dialogue is focused on the individuals taking part drawing on the thinking and learning of all the participants in order to develop their own. It is employing talk, and dialogue in particular, as a learning tool used by children rather than as a teaching strategy used by teachers. Some teachers who have been involved in working towards a dialogic classroom have noted that an element of this approach that may be challenging for teachers is that it is unpredictable and involves teachers relinquishing control. We believe this perceived relinquishing of control is a sacrifice worth making in the interests of better learning.

The Assessment for Learning Strategy (DCSF, 2008) reinforces the need for learning through talk. Many of the self-evaluation statements, to help teachers review their practice in Assessment for Learning (AfL), focus on high-quality talk, much of which needs to be independent of the teacher. In each of the four sections of the continuum – focusing, developing, establishing and enhancing – learning through talk features strongly, both in terms of what children will be able to do and how teachers should facilitate this. These statements range from, 'some are confident to contribute to discussions' to 'there is a classroom buzz: children initiate and lead whole class discussions; group discussions are self determined and governed' (p. 17). Minimal teacher interventions are the desirable outcome following teacher-structured work to enhance children's skills. We hope that this book and the teaching programme it recommends will help teachers and their schools in the implementation of the new strategy by developing teachers' and children's talk skills in support of the continuum criteria.

How to use the book

In order for teachers to make best use of this book, all the workshop activities may be photocopied and we have provided video exemplar material that can be accessed via the publisher's web link. An icon will appear when video material is relevant to the workshop. This material has been used with Year Four and Five children in two schools in West Sussex. However, we believe it could be adapted for use throughout the primary years and have worked with teachers from the Foundation Stage to Key Stages 3 and 4, all of whom have been able to take ideas from it forward into their own settings.

Much of the material provided has no exact curriculum match, as we wanted practitioners to be able to make it fit their needs. Those using the book may prefer to develop their own resources, linked to their curriculum content but we hope the exemplars provided will enable them to do this more confidently. We advocate the use of a 'scaffolded' teaching approach, with use of adult modelling, which teachers will be familiar with through their work with the Primary National Strategy. This approach helps children to develop the skills that will allow them to work productively and independently, freeing the teacher to focus attention on teaching specific children, confident that group talk skills are such that quality outcomes will ensue.

In order to develop the confident learners needed for attainment to be raised, we suggest following the teaching programme in order, although pace may vary according to participants' previous experience.

Each chapter introduces a talk skill beginning with participation and collaboration, leading to building on and extending talk, then making positive challenges and finally resolving and reaching agreement. The programme ends with a section on reflection. Resource 8.1 gives a summary of these six skills. Within each chapter we outline a series of workshops to enable children to raise their awareness of the skills and then practise them. We used a different colour scheme for each set of talk skill resources, so that the children were quickly able to identify those they needed at any given time to develop or consolidate a particular talk skill. We would recommend you use colour when making your own sets. Each skill has an accompanying set of phrase and prompt cards. Summaries of these are given in Resources 8.2 to 8.7. These cards should remain accessible to children at all times, so that they are able to use them in any task where they feel a reminder is necessary.

One scenario is used throughout the book as a means of putting new skills into practice. This takes the form of a voyage to, followed by shipwreck on, an uninhabited island. The final workshop in most chapters revisits the island, setting a problem solving activity for children where the new skill must be used to survive on the island.

Although the aim of the original research project was to improve children's ability to learn independently through quality talk, it had benefits across school life. Staff responsible for children in the playground noticed their ability to sort out disagreements improved markedly. Other teachers noted how children applied the skills they had learned in every aspect of their work and play. Children were able to use the phrases they had learned in a range of contexts and, while the original project had taken place in a Year Four and Five class, the talk of all children in the school improved through contact with these 'experts'.

Participation

How can we enable children to participate and why is it important for effective talk?

An effective learning dialogue, by its very definition, involves more than one participant. (The exception to this is the internal dialogue we describe in Workshop Three.) It is therefore crucial to find ways to enable all children to feel confident in participating in talk activities, if effective learning dialogue is to be the outcome for everyone rather than just a minority. Our experience tells us that some children find participation difficult and that other children, who do not share that difficulty, are not always able to empathise with, or encourage, their less confident peers, as they simply do not recognise the challenges they face.

Photo 1 Participation. Are all the group participating?

This chapter sets out how to enable all children to reach the stage where they feel confident and secure enough to take part in, and contribute to, learning dialogues with their peers. It links very closely with the next chapter, Collaboration and the development of Ground Rules.

Figure 1.1 outlines what the children need to learn in order to be able to participate.

Be aware of their own emotions and the emotions of others around them	Understand the impact of these emotions on how confident we feel to participate
Understand we all need to participate and share ideas	Be able to stay on task

Figure 1.1 What the children need to learn in order to be able to participate.

Introduction to the participation workshops

The following five workshops present ideas for a range of simple games and activities, designed to develop children's awareness of their own and others' emotions and help them to understand the impact of these emotions in group talk situations, including how confidence to participate can be affected. Some of the activities are designed as whole class, shared activities and some for small groups, with or without adult participation. Where adults do participate, they should act as an equal group member, while being aware of their role in modelling appropriate responses. We have found mixed ability groupings work well in these activities.

- **Workshop One** is about raising awareness of a range of emotions and feelings. It involves identifying and recognising some of the emotions that might be experienced when working and talking with others in groups.

- **Workshop Two** is about raising awareness of the consequences of these emotions on group dynamics and the effect that each emotion might have on enabling confident participation within the group.

- **Workshop Three** focuses on developing an internal dialogue that can help children to stop and think about how they are participating and the effect this may have on others.

- **Workshop Four** is about collating phrases that help children to participate. We provide a series of prompt and phrase cards that can be used throughout the activities in this and the following chapters.

- **Workshop Five** introduces an expedition to an island through a problem solving activity designed to enable all children to participate in a learning dialogue.

Workshop One: Raising awareness of our emotions and feelings when talking with others

Identifying and naming our emotions and feelings working in a group

Using photographs

Work with a small group of children. Take a series of photographs that portray the range of emotions the children may experience when working in a group. Look at the photographs as a whole class activity and discuss how each child in the photographs feels. Try to allocate a named emotion to each child. Photographs 1.2 to 1.7 show six photographs of children taken after an eventful playtime, and were used with a class to discuss how each child was feeling.

Examples of other photographs we used with pupils are shown at the start of each chapter of this book. However, we suggest using photographs of your own class to engage and motivate the children.

Complete cartoon faces

In pairs, children should discuss the facial expressions and body language associated with each emotion discussed in activity one and then complete a cartoon face for each emotion (see Figure 1.2). Teachers could ask the children to start spotting expressions and body language in the playground, when shopping or on the television and start an emotions board, where children can log their 'spots'! This extends their understanding of the range of contexts where any given emotion can be experienced. (Resource 8.8 gives some examples of cartoon faces.)

Dice game

The numbers 1–6 on a die are linked to six emotions.

Figure 1.3 gives an example.

In turn the die is rolled and the roller explains what would make them experience the shown emotion when working in a group. For example, if the die landed on 'Sad', a child may comment that they feel sad when they cannot get a turn to speak.

Photo 1.2 Happy

Photo 1.3 Sad

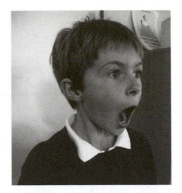

Photo 1.4 Surprised

Photo 1.5 Angry

Photo 1.6 Scared

Photo 1.7 Jealous

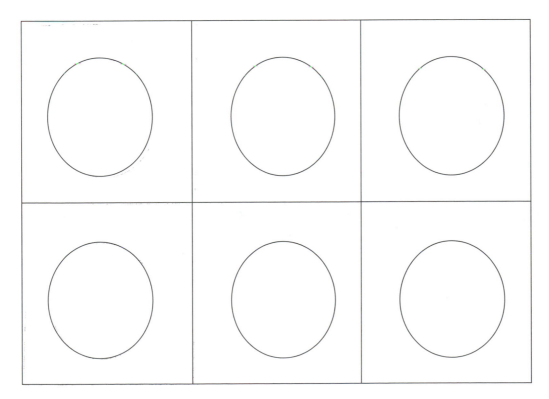

Figure 1.2 Cartoon face emotions grid.

Dice Game:

1. Happy
2. Sad
3. Angry
4. Scared
5. Surprised
6. Jealous

Figure 1.3 Dice game emotions.

| Happy | Sad | Scared |
| Angry | Surprised | Jealous |

Figure 1.4 Charades emotion cards.

Recognising emotions

Non-verbal charades: One child picks an emotion card (see Figure 1.4) from a hat and has to use facial expressions and body language to enable the rest of the class to work out what the emotion is. The better the children get at this, the more subtle they become with their facial expressions and body language, which improves their skills in recognising the full range of emotions during subsequent activities.

Emotions Bingo (linked to how they might feel talking in groups)
Each child is given a board (Figure 1.5) and asked to draw four of their emotion cartoon faces (see earlier activity) on the four blank faces in the bingo grid.

One class member reads out a scenario card (Figure 1.6), and if a child feels the responding emotion is on their card, they cover it with a counter. The first child to cover all their boxes and be able to justify why each is covered is the winner.

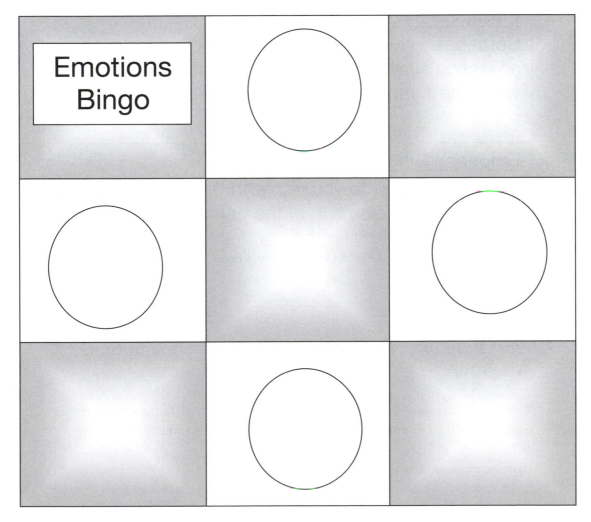

Figure 1.5 Emotions Bingo grid.

Participation

Emotions Bingo Scenario:
Someone in your group says, 'You aren't explaining yourself very well. What do you actually mean?'

Emotions Bingo Scenario:
Someone in your group says to you, 'No that's a useless idea. Be quiet.'

Emotions Bingo Scenario:
Someone in your group says, 'Oh yes, I hadn't thought of that.'

Emotions Bingo Scenario:
Someone in your group who has disagreed with you all lesson suddenly says to you, 'That's the best idea we've had yet, I think we should all agree on that.'

Emotions Bingo Scenario:
The person next to you sits with their back to you so you can't even see two of the people in your group.

Figure 1.6 Examples of scenarios for the Emotions Bingo.

Workshop Two: How should we express our emotions in a group?

This workshop develops the children's understanding of the relationship between emotions, reactions and the consequences of these reactions.

Consequences dominos
Small groups play dominoes where the domino cards include scenarios (Figure 1.7), reactions and consequences. Only when children can justify how a card links to the previous one can it be laid. The team to lay all their cards first are the winners.

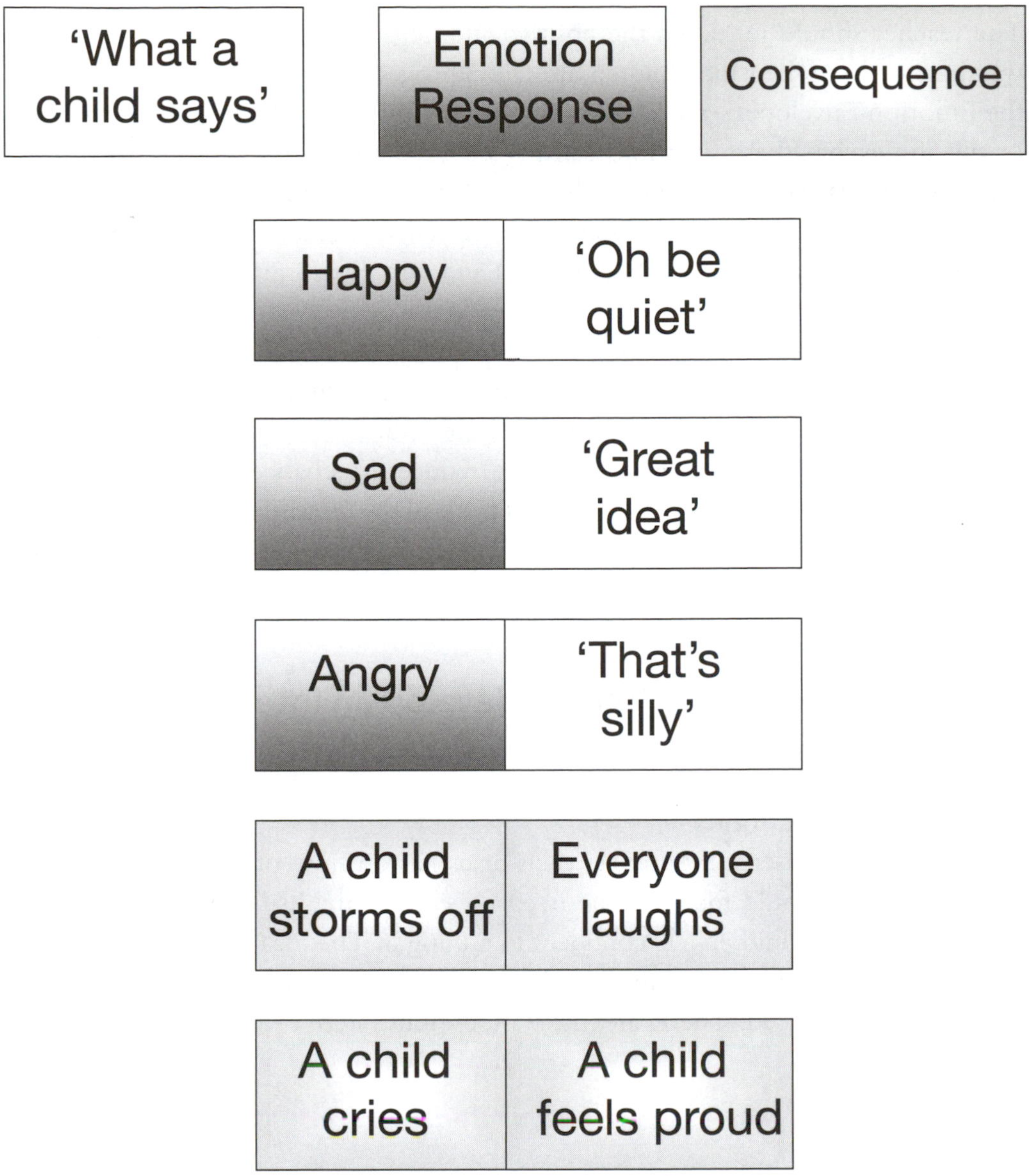

| 'What a child says' | Emotion Response | Consequence |

| Happy | 'Oh be quiet' |

| Sad | 'Great idea' |

| Angry | 'That's silly' |

| A child storms off | Everyone laughs |

| A child cries | A child feels proud |

Figure 1.7 Examples of domino cards.

Emotion	Possible causes	Bad reaction and consequences	Good reaction and consequences

Figure 1.8 Emotions Consequence chart.

Role-play cards

The teacher should jot down the positive and negative situations that can happen within the class when the children are talking together (or use situations given in the Emotion Envelopes – see later in this chapter). With no reference made to names or specific events, these situations can be used as a basis for setting up some role-plays in the classroom, with either the teacher and TA in the role, or even a group of children. The class can then discuss how they would react in that situation, what might happen next, any possible outcomes and why these outcomes might occur.

Consequences chart

The teacher should lead a class dialogue to investigate the possible causes of each emotion and their consequences in given situations. The effect of reacting too quickly or badly, and what can be done to reduce the chances of this happening, should form the focus for discussion. This can be recorded on an Emotions Consequences chart (Figure 1.8) that can be referred to as children learn to manage their group work.

Workshop Three: How can we develop an internal dialogue?

Three step traffic lights

The class should discuss the impact each of us has on how other people feel. Part of the dialogue should focus on the need for each individual to play their part in a group, so that all children feel confident in joining in. The idea of having an internal dialogue, where individuals can stop, think and talk to themselves before reacting should be introduced. There are three steps illustrated below that might help children:

1 Stop and count to five.

2 Think about my reactions and the consequences.

3 Plan my best action and carry it out.

These steps can be linked to traffic lights (Goleman, 1995: 276) which should be prominently displayed, so that when a child is about to react to something that is said, they can use the lights to stop and consider what to do. (For an example, see Figure 1.9.)

Emotion envelopes

Teachers should provide paper and envelopes so that the children can note incidents where they used the traffic lights to help them consider their response. Children can then post the envelopes in a class postbox to ensure anonymity. The teacher should periodically empty the box and share some of the examples with the class. The focus here is on internal dialogue and how individuals react; it is not about blaming others. A sign on the postbox that says 'No names. No blame', can stop it being used to get others into trouble!

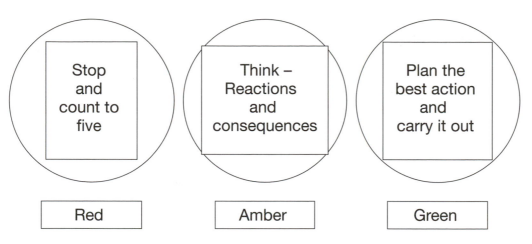

Figure 1.9 Step traffic lights.

Workshop Four: Prompt and phrase cards

While being introduced to and being given opportunities to practise the new talk skills in this book, the children will find it useful to have some prompts and phrases to help them structure what to say. Throughout the book we provide prompt cards (boxes) and phrase cards (speech bubbles) for each new skill. The cards can be used in all the remaining activities in the book. The following are a set used by a class of Year Four and Five children (see Figure 1.10). The prompt cards were provided for them but they devised their own phrase cards. The cards should be printed off and laminated, so that each pair or group always have a set to refer to. When using the cards during their talk, the children can put small counters on a phrase each time they use it during the dialogue and totals can be worked out for each pair or group. The children enjoy quantifying their developing skills in this way and the importance of the phrases is reinforced through reflection on their use.

Workshop Five: Planning an expedition to an island

This workshop introduces the expedition to an uninhabited island that becomes a recurring theme throughout the workshops. The children should work in groups of four and be given a specified time limit in which to pack a bag for the expedition. Each group member has to participate by choosing two items to pack that meet with the approval of the whole group. It is useful to provide either cards with the names and drawings of the objects on, or provide the objects themselves for the group to handle and move around while they discuss their ideas. An example of this problem is shown in Video 1 on the website, and shows the group talk before any skills had been introduced.

Prompt cards:

Participation: Put forward one of my ideas	Participation: Take part in the dialogue

Participation: Make sure everyone is on task

Phrase cards:

> What I think is...

> Are we all concentrating?

> One of my ideas is...

> Let's all...

Figure 1.10 Prompt and phrase cards.

Unexplored islands.....

In the news recently was the discovery of some **unexplored**, **uninhabited** islands. You have been asked to join a group of scientists to sail to these islands to investigate the water and water habitats.

You do not have long to pack.

You each have a rucksack, which can hold 2 items – but what do you take with you?

You are allowed to pack 8 of the following items altogether as a group:

- Compass
- Maps
- Matches
- Chocolate
- Drink water bottle
- Money
- Pen and notepad
- First aid kit
- Camera
- Tent
- Sun cream
- Cutlery
- Sleeping bag
- Magnifying glass
- Plates
- Reading book

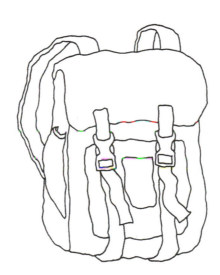

Food is being taken separately on the ship.

Figure 1.11 Unexplored islands.

Participation

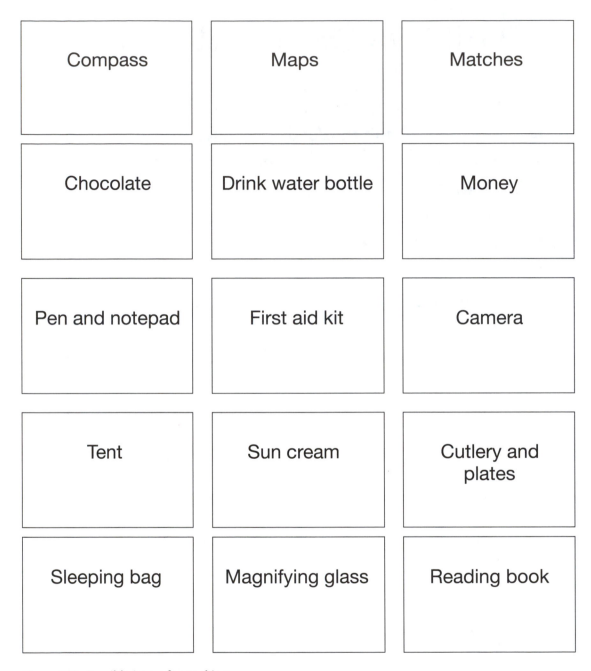

Compass	Maps	Matches
Chocolate	Drink water bottle	Money
Pen and notepad	First aid kit	Camera
Tent	Sun cream	Cutlery and plates
Sleeping bag	Magnifying glass	Reading book

Figure 1.12 Possible items for packing.

CHAPTER 2

Collaboration

How can we enable children to collaborate and why is it important for effective talk?

The ability to collaborate is the second skill that has to be developed in order for children to talk effectively with each other. Collaboration demands that children work together and cooperate with each other. Neither of these skills is necessarily easy for them. In classrooms children often work as individuals while sitting within a group, rather than collaborate to complete a task where all group members must contribute to a successful conclusion. However, if children are to develop an effective learning dialogue then each child has an individual and group responsibility for the talk and the task in hand. Individually, they have a responsibility to participate and collaborate in a positive way and as a group member they must make sure that the entire group share in the dialogue as participants with equal status.

Photo 2.1 Collaboration. Is this group collaborating? How do you know?

Figure 2.1 outlines what the children need to learn in order to be able to collaborate with each other to extend the talk.

Work together to clarify and plan what to do	**Use active listening skills**
Encourage others to participate to ensure everyone contributes	**Respect others and understand that they may have a different viewpoint**

Figure 2.1 What the children need to learn in order to be able to collaborate.

In order for the children to collaborate effectively we believe that ground rules need to be introduced. The majority of research investigating the use of ground rules has made a positive link between their use and children's learning through talk (Mercer, 1995; DfES, 2004a; Alexander, 2006). However, Lambirth (2006) warns against the tendency to produce what he describes as 'Mary Poppins' rules; rules that are too good to be true. Our research supported the use of ground rules to help children work within a climate where dialogue between them is both accepted and promoted. However, we advocate the use of a range of rules, which can be used to 'pick and mix' for any given task (see the suggestions in the workshops). The children who took part in the project certainly found them useful and, encouragingly, chose wisely and later began to revise the 'rules' as they became more confident talkers. This ensured that any 'Mary Poppins' rules devised in the initial stages were refined as the children's understanding of how the rules operated in a variety of contexts developed.

Our Talk Plan

Listen to others and think before speaking.

Be positive and patient.

Treat each other with respect, and think about others feelings.

Make sure everyone is included and share ideas together.

Be prepared to reach an agreement.

Figure 2.2 One group's ground rules.

It is important to involve the children in the development of their own set of ground rules, so that everyone has a fair and equal status, whatever their ability or social and cultural background. Fisher (2003: 179) notes that, with the children deciding on the group rules themselves, they are likely to differ between classes and will reflect the personalities and backgrounds of the children in each class. Different classes may choose different names for their rules. For example, the children who took part in the research project chose 'Our Talk Plan'. Figure 2.2 shows an example of one group's talk plan, put together as the result of their dialogue.

With a little practice the children start to apply the rules to their group talk and when asked about the use of the rules, they appear to value them. For example, a Year Five boy, Matt, said, 'It helped because it reminded me how to work in a group', and Lewis, a Year Four boy, wrote, 'The talk plan helped me because I could keep looking at it.' In particular, it appeared to help the children who struggled when working in a group. For example, Sam from Year Five, a boy who soon got aggressive in group upsets, explained, 'I think the talk plan helps me with my temper.'

Introduction to the collaboration workshops

The following four workshops offer suggestions for developing a set of ground rules that can be used in all talk activities, alongside ideas for encouraging effective collaboration by ensuring every child has the opportunity to contribute.

- **Workshop One** outlines ways of developing a class and group set of ground rules for talk.

- **Workshop Two** provides three activities that encourage the group to check that everyone has participated and collaborated.

- **Workshop Three** provides a collection of prompt and phrase cards that can be used throughout the activities.

- **Workshop Four** is a problem solving activity based on the uninhabited island.

Workshop One: How to develop a class set of ground rules for talk

Begin by asking the class why they might need a set of rules for talking. The aim is to help them understand that the rules they devise should result in everyone being able to participate and collaborate equally. The following activities are designed to lead to an agreed set of rules.

Pairs sticky note challenge

The process starts with time for each child to think of a few rules that they want to have considered. These are then shared with a talk partner and up to five agreed rules are selected and each is written on a separate sticky note.

Photo 2.2 Pair ground rules

Photo 2.3   Group ground rules

Photo 2.4   Class ground rules

Groups of four – top five challenge

Two talk pairs come together and share their sticky notes. The group of four then have to decide on their top five ideas and write them on cards to put forward to the class.

Class voting to produce an agreed class list

The class then sit in a circle with all their cards. Each group reads out one of their cards and it is matched with any cards from other groups that share similar content. These are then compared to decide which card is the best way of explaining that rule. That card is then stuck onto a large sheet or board. This is repeated for all the cards until the class has a sheet of agreed statements. The sheet is then reviewed for any repetitions or omissions. The agreed rules are then typed out and the class decide on a name for their list.

Group top five list

The class list may contain anywhere between eight and fourteen rules; too many for a group to use at any one time. However, by sticking individual rules to the sheet using Velcro, each group can select the five rules they consider best match the task in hand. The class rules can be modified with additions and deletions as groups learn to work together and reflect on how helpful the rules are. However, as individual children and groups develop at different rates, this pick and mix method enables the children to select rules that are appropriate to them and their rate of progress without any loss of self-esteem.

Workshop Two: How to encourage everyone to participate and collaborate

Tick or cross?

A group of four is given a dilemma to discuss (see Figure 2.3 for suggestions). A card is given to each child in the group. One card has a cross on it and three cards have ticks. The children keep their picks secret. The child with the cross card should be instructed not to participate and collaborate as fully as the others. The aim of the game is for the group to work out which child holds the cross card as quickly as possible.

The missing link

Each child in the group is given a card with a separate piece of information and a happy or unhappy face on it. All the pieces of information are needed to complete the dialogue successfully. The child with the unhappy face should be told not to collaborate fully. The rest of the group has to try out strategies to get that child to contribute, in order to ascertain the missing piece of information and successfully complete the task. Figure 2.4 gives an example based around some subject content, and an example based around a social problem.

Tick or Cross Card 1	Tick or Cross Card 2
You see your best friend cheating in a test. What should you do?	A close friend is bullying you. What should you do?

Figure 2.3 Possible dilemmas to dicuss.

Example One: Based around some subject content.

We are told we must have a sustainable future	What can we each do to help this happen?
There are lots of little things we can do to be sustainable	Sustainable means using without using up

Example Two: Based around a social problem.

What happened and what can be done about it?	Ann's teacher noticed she has been really quiet recently
Ann was hit and pushed over at playtime	Ann's friend Ash gets angry really quickly when she doesn't get her own way

Figure 2.4 Example One: Based around some subject contents.
Example Two: Based around a social problem.

Missing Link Dialogue

The teacher should lead a class dialogue to investigate which strategies were successful in encouraging the fourth child to collaborate. For example, the teacher may ask questions such as:

● Tell me how you helped to involve child four.

● Which strategies worked best of all?

● Were there any strategies you used that didn't help at all?

A list of useful phrases can be collated for future use and the dialogue may well lead into a discussion of the value of open and closed questions, something the children will need to be aware of and that comes up later in this book.

Workshop Three: Prompt and phrase cards

The following set of phrase cards were devised by the children in the research project (see Figure 2.5). The prompt cards were given to the children first and they then devised their own phrase cards in speech bubbles. As in the participation workshops, we advise printing and laminating the sets of cards on a specific colour so that each pair or group have a copy to refer to whenever they need them.

Prompt cards:

Collaboration:	Collaboration:
Listen & try to understand what others are saying	Make it clear what you have to do. Plan what to do to solve this problem.
Collaboration:	Collaboration:
Have your say, but don't let anyone dominate	Make sure everyone in the group has spoken.

Phrase cards:

I wonder what .... thinks.

Are we all clear what we have to do?

Have we all given an idea?

What should we all be doing?

Figure 2.5 Prompt and phrase cards.

Workshop Four: On the uninhabited island

The following two scenarios demand that the children collaborate in order to solve the problem. Both continue the story started in the previous chapter and are set on the uninhabited island following a shipwreck. The first scenario provides a context for the class to make decisions about their ground rules, as they need to decide how they will communicate with each other on their deserted island (see Figure 2.6). The second scenario requires a group of four children to collaborate with each other to allocate jobs on the island. As the problem involves two boys and two girls, it results in an interesting dialogue about equal and fair status for both sexes and requires the group to use the ground rules (see Figure 2.7).

Photo 2.5 Who does the washing up?

Photo 2.6 Learning to build a fire

Shipwreck

We have landed on an undiscovered, uninhabited island. We must work together in order to survive. There will be many problems to face.

How are we going to work together?
How should we talk to each other when working in our groups to solve the problems?

Figure 2.6 Shipwreck.

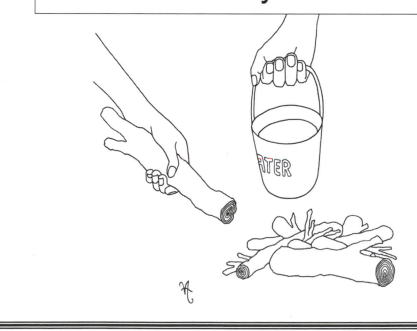

Jobs to do!

There are four of you shipwrecked on your island: two girls and two boys but no adults.

What sort of jobs do you need to do to survive? Who should do which jobs? Why?

Figure 2.7 Jobs to do.

CHAPTER 3

Build-on and extend ideas

What is building on and why is it important for effective talk?

Within whole class and group discussions, children often respond in very short contributions of less than ten words. When carrying out research in two schools with Year Four and Five children, the authors discovered that, during group talk, 96 per cent of the individual responses were of fewer than ten words. This echoes the findings of Hardman, Smith and Wall (2003) in their review of interactive teaching in the Literacy Hour, where they found 70 per cent of exchanges were three words or less. They also found only 4 per cent of the children studied for the review extended points made by other children.

Photo 3.1 Build-on

When listening to group talk, a series of monologues can often be overheard, where each individual says what he or she thinks without ever listening to or responding to others. Therefore, no real dialogue is taking place and, with no chains of talk or enquiry, the talk is unlikely to extend learning. Children need to learn how to build on to their own and each other's ideas to extend their talk. This will allow deeper learning to take place, as the children question and expand on the ideas put forward in the dialogue and sustain the talk needed to reach an agreement. Figure 3.1 shows what children need to learn in order to build-on and extend the talk.

Add more detail to their own or others' ideas	Use questions to extend the dialogue
Give longer responses and sustain ideas over a sequence of responses	Give feedback to previous contributions

Figure 3.1 What the children need to learn in order to be able to build-on.

The following extracts of children talking in a group of four illustrate how developing the skills of building on qualitatively alter the effectiveness of the talk. They show clearly how the same group of children have started to learn how to listen to each other and respond to what is being said, following the introduction of the building on workshops.

Extract One (Table 3.1)
This extract records the talk before the children have learned the skills of building on and answers the question: We are going on an expedition to an unexplored island. What should we take with us?

36

Table 3.1 Extract One

Nathan	Sally	Orla	Matt
We need chocolate			
	No	No we don't need chocolate (loudly)	
Orla!			Yes we do
	Oh for goodness sake		
			We do need cutlery (loudly)
	We don't need cutlery	We need water	

Extract Two (Table 3.2)

This extract records the same group after they had learned the building on skills. Shipwrecked alone on the island, they discover that some of the food supplies are missing. Could it be their friend stealing them?

Table 3.2 Extract Two (*continued overleaf*)

Nathan	Sally	Orla	Matt
		So do we all know what we should be doing?	
Yes	Yes		Yes
	Well he could be lying so maybe what we could do is to hide behind the bushes or around the food store to see if he is actually taking the food first before you tell anyone else.		
I disagree with that because that friend might get slightly hurt. Your friend might think you are spying on them or accusing them.			
		And the other two might gang up on him.	
			If you told them.

Table 3.2 Extract Two *(continued)*

Nathan	Sally	Orla	Matt
		Yes if you told them, and he might feel very left out. Which wouldn't be very nice.	
We just need to stop him doing it. So maybe we mention we all wanted to do something like that. Think about everyone else and we are all hungry.			
			Yes
		If you ate all the food everyone would suffer	
Yes. Everyone would suffer if all the food had run out.			
		Yes everyone would suffer, not just you, because you would run out of food and they would run out of food. So if the food went quicker you might just end up on the island just by yourself …	

Introduction to the building on workshops

The following workshops provide a series of activities that will help raise children's awareness of how to build-on and extend ideas and teach them how to use these skills in their dialogues.

- **Workshop One** focuses on raising awareness of the need to build-on and extend talk, through the evaluation of role-plays and videos.

- **Workshop Two** provides prompt and phrase cards that can be used throughout the following activities.

- **Workshop Three** outlines four activities that can be used to develop aspects of this new talk skill.

- **Workshop Four** gives some examples of activities that can be used within group dialogues to practise this new talk skill.

- **Workshop Five**, set on the uninhabited island, requires the children to use their build-on skills and extend their ideas in order to solve two problems.

Workshop One: Raising awareness through the use of role-play and video

Evaluating role-play is a good starting strategy, as it means the children are free to discuss what is happening without having to comment on themselves or their friends. The role-play participants can be any two people, such as the teacher and TA, or the teacher and a pre-rehearsed child. In addition, short videos can be taken of rehearsed 'bad' dialogues between other people in the school community. The children really enjoy watching staff 'do it all wrong'!

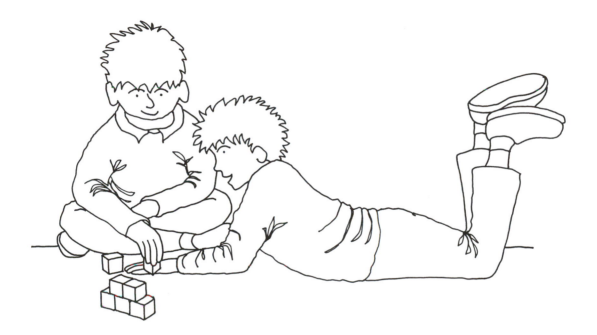

The first range of role-plays should show two people talking without responding to each other. A good focus is to discuss a recent story in the news, where both participants give their own view, or comment on their own experiences linked to the story, without responding at all to each other. These bad examples should be discussed with the children to reveal that neither person's thinking has changed by the end of the dialogue and no 'common understanding' has been reached. The class can then discuss how this dialogue might be improved.

The second range of role-plays should then show two people building on to and extending their own or their partner's talk; ideas are developed through asking questions of each other, adding more detail to what has been said, and offering alternative viewpoints to discuss.

The children should then discuss the differences between the two dialogues and draw attention to the talk strategies and the phrases that enabled the improved dialogue to happen.

Prompt cards

Build and Extend:	Build and Extend:
Give longer answers and have chains of dialogue	Make sure my my ideas are clear and I don't use vague words
Build and Extend:	Build and Extend:
Offer a different reason why	Respond and add to someone else's idea

Phrase cards

I agree because...

I disagree because...

What do you think?

I like that idea

Figure 3.2 Prompt and phrase cards.

Learning through Talk, Routledge © Heather Luxford and Lizzie Smart 2009

Workshop Two: Prompt and phrase cards

In order to help structure what to say, a class of Year Four and Five children devised the following prompt and phrase cards (Figure 3.2). They were first given the set of cards illustrated earlier in this chapter, that outline what children need to learn in order to be able to build on effectively. The children then worked together to devise these prompt and phrase cards, with each group producing a set of phrases to use in their dialogues. During the group dialogues that followed, each time a child used one of the phrases they would turn the relevant phrase card over. Children enjoyed seeing the physical evidence of their development in this way and the activity worked well to embed knowledge of the phrases.

Workshop Three: Activities to practise the new skill

'Talk Triangles': Focus – How to use questions to extend talk

This task can be carried out in groups of three, when one child takes the role of the speaker, one the questioner and one the observer. Each child is given a role card (see Figure 3.3 and Resource 8.9).

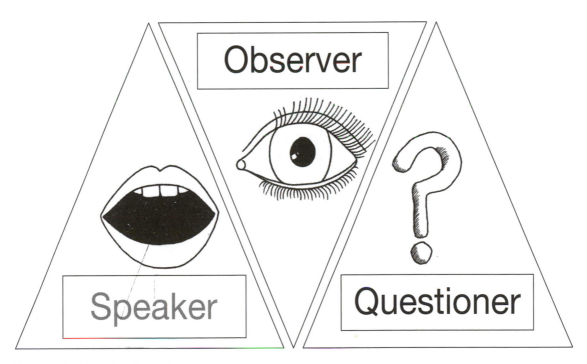

Figure 3.3 Talk Triangle cards.

Possible topics for a dialogue:

- A favourite hobby …
- A club I attend …
- A memorable holiday …
- My best day at school …
- My best Christmas or birthday …
- A time when I was scared …
- My favourite TV programme …
- *Anything you want to talk about …*

Figure 3.4 Topics for a dialogue.

A topic is then given for the speaker to talk about. Examples are given in Figure 3.4.

The job of the questioner is to ask questions that elicit as much detail as possible about the speaker's topic. The observer notes down the types of questions that were asked and evaluates how effective they were in eliciting detail. Roles can be rotated round the group and at the end of the activity a plenary dialogue can take place, where children develop their understanding through sharing observations. It should become apparent that open questions are much better at extending the talk than closed questions.

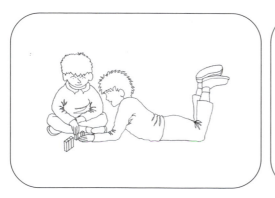

Figure 3.5 Build-on cards.

Build-on cards: Focus – How to add detail to the previous contribution

A set of cards (see Figure 3.5) can be made for each pair or group. The teacher should then provide a dialogue topic for each group: For example, about something that has happened at school recently. Each time a building on phrase is used, the user picks up a card. At the conclusion of the dialogue, totals can be tallied to see which individual used the most phrases, or which pair or group did. (See Resource 8.10, and an example of this activity on Video 4 on the website.)

Chain us up: Focus – How to extend the chain of talk

Each group needs an old ball of wool or string. They then carry out a group dialogue on a given topic. The first person that speaks holds the end of the wool and when someone responds to their initial contribution, the ball of wool gets passed on to that person. This second person holds on to the wool while speaking, and when a third person extends the talk further the ball of wool is passed on, while the second speaker continues to hold tightly to their end. At the end of the dialogue the wool will have been passed around the group for each chain of responses and will reveal all the chains. The children loved this activity and the complex 'webs' that resulted from their dialogues. (An example of this activity is given in Video 5 on the website.)

Photo 3.2 Chain us up

Photo 3.3 Squiggle game

Build-on squiggle game

This is a quick, fun activity to do. Before the activity, the teacher draws a squiggle of any shape, using a coloured pen, anywhere on an A3 sheet. Enough sheets for each group in the class need to be provided. Each group of four is then given one of these A3 sheets of paper, with a pen of a different colour. The group have to work together to build-on each other's ideas to convert the squiggle into an A3 picture. At the end of the activity they can then tell a story based on their picture, by taking it in turns to build-on the previous contribution until the story is told. (A video example of a group of teachers, role-playing how not to do this activity, can be found on the website.)

Workshop Four: Using the new skill in groups to discuss dilemmas

Once the children have understood all the new skills needed to build-on and extend their talk, they can apply them to discuss dilemmas in their groups. Some examples are given in Figure 3.6. The children may still need to have the phrase cards on the table to support them throughout this activity.

Build-on talk card 1 What would life be like if we all looked the same?	Build-on talk card 2 You find out that someone is saying unkind things about your best friend. What should you do?
Build-on talk card 3 If you could only eat five foods for the next six months, what would they be and why?	Build-on talk card 4 What would happen if the children appointed the teachers in their school?
Build-on talk card 5 You find a £20 note on the path on the way to school. What should you do?	Build-on talk card 6 You've been invited to two friends' birthday parties on the same night. What should you do?

Figure 3.6 Dilemmas for a dialogue.

Workshop five: Three problem-solving tasks set on the uninhabited island

These three tasks provide problems that the group might have to face on their island. In order to solve the problems they will need to build-on each other's ideas and extend their talking and thinking in order to find the best solutions possible. They will have to apply what they have learnt to make best use of the one set of resources given for each of the tasks. By this stage the prompt and phrase cards may not be needed, as the children start to use them automatically. An example of 'Survival' is shown in Video 2 on the website.

45

Survival!

We are trying to survive on our uninhabited island.
We have just discovered one bag washed up on the beach.

Inside the bag you find:

- **2 clothes pegs**
- **1 cotton bud**
- **1 piece of card and paper**
- **2 paper clips**
- **1 straw**
- **1 cocktail stick**

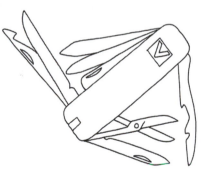

You have 10 minutes to use these objects to make a group tool/ penknife to use on the island. You need to be able to explain what each part is for.

Figure 3.7 Survival!

Bridge the gap!

You are getting low on wood for your fire … it cannot go out. There is a forest on the other side of the river but you need to cross this river to be able to carry the wood back to your camp.

You can use all the resources given to you to build a 'bridge' to get across the river and back again.

Figure 3.8 Bridge the gap!

Rags!

We have been on the island many weeks now and our clothes have become rags.

You need to design a new outfit for one member of your group using just the magazines, newspaper and masking tape provided.
It must be suitable for your island.
What 'accessories' could you add to make it good for living on an island?

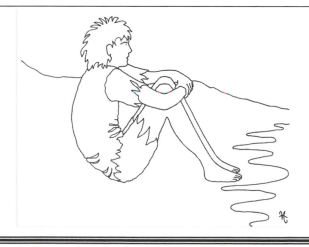

Figure 3.9 Rags!

Positive challenge

How can we enable children to challenge each other in a positive way and why is it important for effective talk?

If a child's view is just accepted without being challenged, then there is a real danger that the talk has not been used to extend group or individual understanding, and it may fall into a series of monologues (Barnes and Todd, 1995: 159). In order to extend their understanding and learning, children need to be confident in expressing and justifying their own viewpoint and in challenging the viewpoints and listening to the justifications of others. This is the type of dialogue through which learning develops.

Photo 4.1 Challenge. Are these children challenging appropriately? How do you know?

There are many dialogues that take place in classrooms that allow children to express their thinking. However, as Fisher (2003: 136) states, these dialogues do not always provide the cognitive challenge that is needed to extend children's thinking. If a child's view is challenged, they have to clarify and justify their viewpoint and when other viewpoints are put forward then these alternative ideas have to be considered. Dialogue that includes these two factors will extend thinking and hence understanding and learning. Our experience tells us that this is a skill many children find difficult to master. They need a lot of practice in both group and class situations if they are to become confident in challenging each other positively.

This series of workshops also comes with a health warning! Children who learn these skills will transfer them to all aspects of their school and home life. It may be advisable to discuss the children's new found skills with the wider school community, as we are aware that not all adults are comfortable with children who challenge, albeit positively.

The composition of a group will influence the group's ability to challenge and be challenged. Friendship groups may work well together but are less likely to challenge each other for fear of unsettling the friendship. One child commented that working in a friendship group was less helpful as she already knew what her close friends thought and felt about most things. Friends certainly are more likely to have similar views, so their knowledge and understanding may be less likely to be challenged. To think more deeply about the task, the participants in the group need to have contrasting or less well-known viewpoints. One Year Five girl, when talking to the video diary, started to show her awareness of needing this mix in the group:

'Our group is a mixture of boys and girls and it's a bit annoying because the boys are usually in competition with the girls and the girls in competition with the boys. But it's not always a bad thing, because you have got to challenge them and try and get to a decision and that's what we've got to work on, I think.'

However, if there is not trust between the group members then they may not all participate. One of the aims of the workshops in this chapter is to develop that necessary trust.

Figure 4.1 shows what children need to learn in order to be able to feel confident to challenge each other to extend the talk.

Ask higher order questions	Ask for clarification
Ask for justification	Challenge and reject viewpoints in a constructive way

Figure 4.1 What the children need to learn in order to be able to challenge.

Introduction to the challenge workshops

The following five workshops provide a range of activities that will help raise awareness and confidence levels and teach children how to use positive challenge to improve the quality of their talk.

- **Workshop One** is about raising awareness of the need to use positive challenge to extend ideas and clarify meaning. It is done through the evaluation of role-play and video.

- **Workshop Two** is about collating phrases that help children to challenge each other. It provides prompt cards that can be used throughout the activities.

- **Workshop Three** outlines three activities that can be used to improve the ability to clarify and justify a viewpoint.

- **Workshop Four** shows how using traffic lights can help children apply this skill in both group and class dialogues.

- **Workshop Five** gives three examples of problems, which are set on the uninhabited island, in which the groups need to challenge each other's ideas in order to reach an agreed resolution.

Workshop One: Raising awareness through the use of role-play and video

The use of an adult role-play is particularly helpful for raising awareness of positive challenge, as children can become quickly upset when challenged in a negative way. An example of such a video is given in Video 8 on the website.

It is of two class teachers and two TAs playing the Squiggle Game (detailed in the previous chapter). The children should use this video to discuss the impact of someone dominating the dialogue and of someone challenging in a negative way.

Workshop Two: Prompt and phrase cards

The children need to understand the meaning of the two key words 'clarify' and 'justify', in order to understand positive challenge. Each pair should be given the task to discover the meaning of these two words and to give an example of each. Their ideas are then transferred onto prompt and phrase cards (Figure 4.2) and each pair practises using these phrases throughout a dialogue; for example, while discussing an environmental issue such as recycling or when we should walk or use the car. They can keep a tally of how often they use each phrase and compare at the end of the dialogue.

Prompt cards:

Positive Challenge:

Ask good, open questions

Positive Challenge:
Challenge others' ideas in a polite and respectful way

Positive Challenge:
Ask for a justification - ask why they think that

Positive Challenge:
Ask for clarification - ask what they mean

Phrase cards:

Why do you think that?

What do you mean by that?

What would happen if?

I'm not sure about that because...

Figure 4.2 Prompt and phrase cards.

Photo 4.2 Who uses each phrase?

Workshop Three: Three activities that can be used to improve the children's ability to clarify and justify a viewpoint

Character Cards

Initially the children find it easier to challenge each other when in the role of fictional characters rather than 'being themselves'. This enables them to challenge with no personal risk of upsetting anyone. The activity involves each child picking a character card (e.g. from nursery rhymes and fairy tales in Figure 4.3 and Resource 8.11, or from television or literature such as *The Simpsons*, *Harry Potter* or *Tracey Beaker*) and becoming that person to imagine how they might react in a dialogue.

To begin with, each pair chooses characters from the same source, such as Little Red Riding Hood and the Big Bad Wolf or Lisa and Bart Simpson and then argue opposing points of view for dilemmas and questions given. For example, when using the following cards in Figure 4.4, each child has to choose the viewpoint that most closely matches their character. (An example of this activity is given in Video 6 on the website.)

Figure 4.3 Fairy tale character cards.

Opposite viewpoint card 1	
Your friend has found £10 on the path and has kept it.	
Viewpoint 1 Hand it in – but where?	Viewpoint 2 Keep it – You don't know who it belongs to.

Opposite viewpoint card 2	
What should you do if you are given too much change in a shop?	
Viewpoint 1 Keep it.	Viewpoint 2 Hand it back.

Opposite viewpoint card 3	
Is it more important to be happy or rich?	
Viewpoint 1 Happy	Viewpoint 2 Rich

Opposite viewpoint card 4	
Is it better to be a child or an adult?	
Viewpoint 1 Child	Viewpoint 2 Adult

Figure 4.4 Opposite viewpoint dialogue cards.

Learning through Talk, Routledge © Heather Luxford and Lizzie Smart 2009

Opposite viewpoint card 5	
A friend lends you a toy and you lose it. Should you buy them a new one?	
Viewpoint 1	Viewpoint 2
Yes	No

Opposite viewpoint card 6	
Would you rather live in India or America?	
Viewpoint 1	Viewpoint 2
India	America

Opposite viewpoint card 7	
Would you rather have a friend who is great fun or one you can trust?	
Viewpoint 1	Viewpoint 2
Great fun	Trust

Opposite viewpoint card 8	
When you grow up would you rather become a teacher or an actor?	
Viewpoint 1	Viewpoint 2
Teacher	Actor

Figure 4.4 *continued* . . .

Learning through Talk, Routledge © Heather Luxford and Lizzie Smart 2009

An extension activity using the character cards is to mix up characters from different stories. For example, the children can explore how Bart Simpson would talk to and challenge the Big Bad Wolf, or how Cinderella would talk to and challenge Tracey Beaker. The children enjoyed playing with the characters and matching them to the different viewpoints.

Opposite viewpoint situations

Once the children are confident, they can revert to being themselves and start discussing situations from the opposite viewpoints in Figure 4.4, using the talk prompts and phrases to help scaffold their talk.

In pairs
To start, the children discuss the Opposite Viewpoint Cards, with each of the pair selecting either viewpoint one or two.

In groups
Green and red traffic lights can be used to indicate each child's own viewpoint within the group (Figure 4.5). A topic is introduced to the class, for example an issue linked to play time such as, 'Younger and older classes should have different play times'. Within the group those that agree with the viewpoint hold up a green card and those that don't hold up a red card (see Figure 4.5).

Each child needs to clarify their own view and then ask for justification of any alternative views in the group. After listening to a range of views on each side, children may change their original view, if the arguments have been powerful enough.

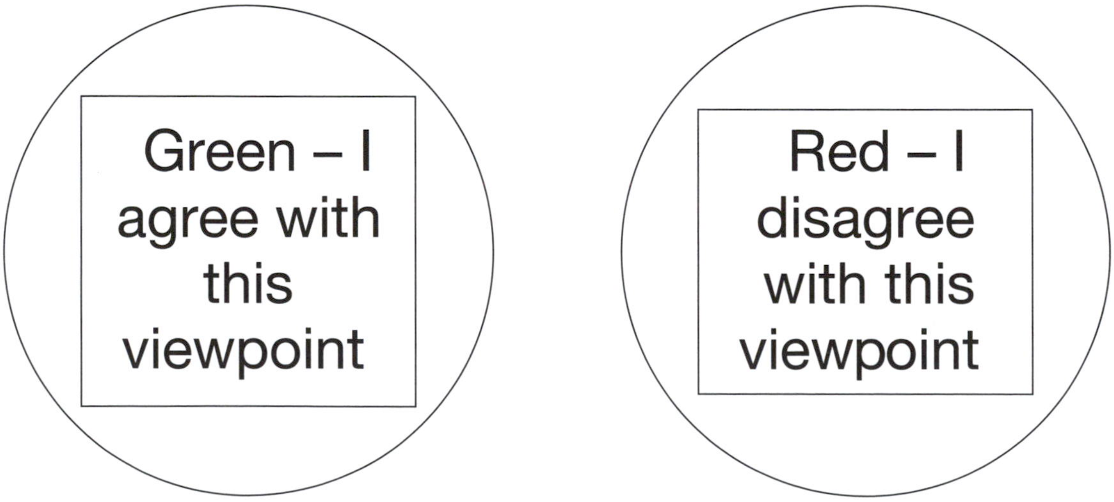

Green – I agree with this viewpoint

Red – I disagree with this viewpoint

Figure 4.5 Group traffic light cards.

Learning through Talk, Routledge © Heather Luxford and Lizzie Smart 2009

In a class

These traffic lights can be used with a whole class. The class need to be in an open space such as the hall or playground. Once a viewpoint is given everyone has to hold up either the green or red traffic light, depending on whether they agree or disagree with the viewpoint. The votes are then counted. Each child then moves around the space and either clarifies their viewpoint with someone with the same colour traffic light as them, or justifies their viewpoint with a person with the opposite colour. A child can change their colour traffic light at any point during the activity, if they are convinced by someone else's argument. At the end, the number of green and red lights are counted and compared with the first tally. At this stage it is helpful to ask the children about their reasons for sticking with or changing their original view. Useful dialogue about the types of arguments that were powerfully made can ensue and this reflection helps in future activities.

News stories

Ask the children to collect a range of news stories linked to a class topic. This can be done through a class News Journal, which children volunteer to take home for a couple of days.

Photo 4.3 The News Journal

They look for interesting news stories from the television, internet, or a local, national or child's newspaper and produce a summary of the story for the class News Journal. These stories can then be used to stimulate debate about real and relevant issues. After choosing a focus story, the class split into groups with different viewpoints. It is helpful to allow some group sharing time at this stage, for children to clarify their ideas with those who hold a similar viewpoint. Following this, the children can debate the issue by asking for clarification and justification of each other's views.

Workshop Four: Extended traffic lights

This workshop focuses on using an extended set of traffic lights to help apply the skill further in both group and class dialogues. Three coloured cards are given to each child: each one represents a point of view (see Figure 4. 6).

These cards can either be used by groups or by the whole class sitting in a circle to discuss a range of topics, dilemmas or 'what if' questions linked to the class topic. A video example (Video 7) is provided on the linked website of a class using the traffic light cards for the first time in a whole class dialogue. The problem being discussed is the Freedom problem illustrated in the next chapter. The aim was for the children to develop chains of responses without constant input from the teacher. (Further discussion of this activity is given on the website.)

Green – I have a new idea I would like to share with everyone

Amber – I would like to agree with and back up what has just been said

Red – I would like to question or disagree with what has just been said

Figure 4.6 Class dialogue traffic light cards.

Workshop Five: The uninhabited island

This workshop provides two examples of problems, set on the uninhabited island, in which the groups need to challenge each other's ideas in order to solve the problem. Both problems are dilemmas that might occur on the island and neither have an obvious answer. Therefore, all viewpoints put forward need to be very clear and justified. An example of 'Missing supplies' is shown in Video 3 on the website.

Missing supplies

You are all very hungry. Food and water supplies are starting to run out on the island, and you are aware food seems to be disappearing.

You spot your best friend sneaking out from where the food is stored.

When you mention it he says that he was just checking it was all there, but you know something else has disappeared.

Your best friend does not get on very well with the other two and you worry how the other two will react if you tell them....

What should you do about it?

Figure 4.7 Missing supplies.

First aid *kit*

A group of four of you and your dog have made it to the island. Your first aid kit has been washed up on the beach, but you have a dilemma. Your dog is sick and the kit contains medicines and bandages that will make him feel more comfortable.

However, one of the group has said that there are not many medicines so you should save them in case one of you falls ill.

What should you do?

Figure 4.8 First aid kit.

CHAPTER 5

Resolve and reach agreement

How can we enable children to resolve their differences and reach an agreement, and why is this important for effective talk?

Most interactions use discussion in some way to share ideas but a dialogue is about reaching a common understanding and reaching an agreed consensus; in other words it is about the negotiation and compromise that allow tasks to move forward to completion rather than go round in ever decreasing circles. Children need to learn to sustain their talk in order to reach an agreement. To do this, they need to learn how to resolve differences without coming to blows!

Photo 5.1   Resolve. How well is this group resolving its difficulties? How do you know?

Table 5.1 Video extract

Harry	David	Jessie	Belinda
		So we're saying we'll share everything and have a day each	
But maybe the boys should chop the wood and catch the fish?		No Harry, we'd already talked about that. Can we please stick to what we had?	
			Agreed
	Yes. Girl, boy, girl, boy, girl, boy …		
		So do we all agree?	So have we all decided?
	Yes	So I think we've decided to …	
Yes, OK, to have one day each			
		Yes	
	So have we decided?		
Yes all agree			Yes
		David agree?	
	Agreed		
		Jessie agree … Yes	
Yes		Harry agree	
		Belinda agree	
			Yes

They will also need plenty of opportunity to practise this skill, especially after learning how to challenge. Our experience shows that pupils find this difficult. After a short group challenge, one boy explained in his talk log that 'we did not do very well because our talk group could not agree after challenging each other.'

The following transcript of a video extract (Table 5.1) shows how one group has started to use their resolving skills. It records the dialogue of a group trying to resolve and reach agreement with the 'Jobs to do' problem explained in Chapter Two. Just as the group started to reach an agreement, one group member proffered an alternative viewpoint. However, the rest of the group were able to challenge him positively before continuing to work together to reach an agreement the whole group were happy with.

Figure 5.1 shows what children need to learn in order to be able to resolve their differences and reach agreement.

Generalise or summarise the ideas	Check for agreement
Bring the task to a conclusion	Reach an agreement

Figure 5.1 What the children need to learn in order to be able to resolve and reach agreement.

Introduction to resolve and reach agreement workshops

The following five workshops offer ideas for a range of simple activities designed to develop children's ability to resolve differences within a group and be able to reach an agreement:

- **Workshop One** focuses on raising awareness of the means to resolve differences and reach an agreement. It is done through the evaluation of role-plays and videos.

- **Workshop Two** is about collating phrases that help children in resolving their differences and reaching an agreement. It provides prompt cards that can be used throughout the following activities.

- **Workshop Three** outlines three activities that can be used to develop generalising or summarising of ideas.

- **Workshop Four** sets out two activities that can be used to develop the children's ability to check for and reach an agreement.

- **Workshop Five** provides three examples of scenarios, set on the uninhabited island, in which the groups need to be able to resolve differences and reach an agreement.

Workshop One: Raising awareness through the evaluation of role-play and video

Some children will find it difficult to accept that they cannot always get their own way in a group, because they struggle to recognise the group's needs above their own. Trying to resolve these differences can lead to stubborn variances of opinion! Videos of role-plays can be shown, with either members of staff or rehearsed children in the roles. As discussed in previous chapters, the dialogue surrounding these role-plays enables groups of children to discuss the issues without any personal involvement or fear of embarrassment.

One role-play could involve a pair, perhaps the class teacher and the TA, or two rehearsed children, discussing a possible solution to a problem faced in the school. One example could be focused on whether games of football should be allowed on the playground every play time. At first the role players contradict and challenge each other without ever agreeing and hence no decision is made. Then they decide they need to compromise and, through further dialogue, are able to find common ground and reach an agreement about what is to be done. Examples of a role-play, where this problem is discussed between a teacher and TA, can be found on the linked website. Evaluating this role-play helps children become aware that all decision-making involves exploring differences and compromising in order to reach an agreed consensus.

Videoing groups talking together can also be useful. When the group have the opportunity to review their video, they can start to recognise at which point they needed to compromise or negotiate and this reflection helps develop appropriate behaviours in their next dialogue.

Workshop Two: Prompt and phrase cards

One Year Four and Five class used the first role-play video of the two adults discussing football at playtime, to discuss how the dialogue would never have reached any agreement. Discussion then followed about what the adults should have done. Next, talk partners tried out the ideas proffered by the whole class until the following four stages were decided upon (Figure 5.2). It was pointed out that if there were disagreements at stage three then the task would need to be discussed again and only after everyone agreed could the final agreement – stage four – be stated.

Prompt cards:

Resolve:	Resolve:
1. Give a summary of what's been said	2. Propose a decision
Resolve:	Resolve:
3. Check whether everyone agrees	4. Give an answer or solution to the problem

Phrase cards:

So what are we all saying?

What do we all agree on?

Do we all agree or shall we discuss it some more?

So we have all decided to ...

Figure 5.2 Prompt and phrase cards.

Workshop Three: Activities that can be used to develop how to generalise or summarise ideas

Hot seating

The notion of hot seating will be familiar to most teachers in primary schools, following its promotion through the Primary National Strategy. In this activity, one child in each group takes on the role of a different character from the same story (a story shared in class, or a familiar film or television programme) in order to discuss characters and their motives. The rest of the group then pose a range of questions to enable them to explore the character's personality and behaviour and their impact on the plot. For example:

How would you describe yourself?

Why did you do that in the story?

How were you feeling at this time?

How should you have behaved when . . . ?

How would this have changed what happened?

Photo 5.2 Hot seating

Who is the most important person in this story and why?

How are you different to . . . in the story?

What are the key events to you in this story?

Why did things happen this way?

Which was the best part of the story for you? Why?

What have you learnt?

What would you do differently next time?

The child in the hot seat then comes out of the role and the group have to summarise the ideas discussed and these summaries are then used in a class dialogue to compare all the characters.

Summary challenge

This task involves children learning how to summarise aspects of learning in the classroom. A summary card (Figure 5.3) is given to one child at the start of a dialogue and the child is later asked to summarise the main points.

Summary Card

Listen carefully to the dialogue and give a brief summary at the end of the main points discussed

Figure 5.3 Individual summary.

Learning through Talk, Routledge © Heather Luxford and Lizzie Smart 2009

Groups could be given a group summary card where they are asked to summarise their own group dialogue, or where they work together to summarise a class dialogue. Groups could also be challenged to summarise a short story told in class, a familiar traditional tale or a news story. This is also a useful strategy for children in developing their storytelling skills, as summarising a story into five or seven parts acts as a prompt for when they tell their own stories.

Jigsaw dialogue

The jigsaw technique was outlined as a talk strategy in the DfES pack *Speaking, Listening, Learning: Working with Children in Key Stages 1 & 2 Handbook* (DfES, 2003b). In the context of this chapter, the strategy could be used as a method for the children to learn to summarise ideas. The class is divided into 'home' groups of four children. Each child in the group selects one of the four areas to be discussed. For example, to extend the class understanding of fair trade, the following four areas could be discussed:

1 Why there is a need for fair trade.

2 The range of fair trade products that can be purchased.

3 The specific example of the banana trade.

4 The countries in the world that produce fair trade products.

Children with the same area to discuss meet in 'expert' groups. These 'expert' groups research their area and plan how to summarise what they have learnt to take back to their 'home' group. The children then return to their 'home' group to share their new area of expertise. The 'home' group listens to one another and asks questions for clarification, until the entire group understands all four areas.

Workshop Four: Activities that can be used to develop the children's ability to check for and reach a joint agreement

Mystery objects

From visiting bric-a-brac shops and car boot sales, it is quite easy to make an inexpensive collection of unusual objects, whose functions are not easily recognisable. This is enjoyable for the teacher in preparation for the tasks!

Each group of children receives one of these objects, wrapped to conceal its features. By using touch, the children explore ideas as to what the object could be, each child building on the previous child's idea. The parcels are opened and the dialogue continues about the age and function of the object. Each group then has to reach an agreement about their object and present their ideas to the rest of class, justifying their decisions.

Photo 5.3   What is the mystery object?

Photo 5.4   Dialogue about the mystery object

Four viewpoint cards

A group receives a dilemma with four different viewpoints on the same topic (Figure 5.4). Each child within the group takes one of the different viewpoints. They are then given a set amount of time to discuss the dilemma, but with each child arguing for their chosen viewpoint. At a given signal from the teacher, the group must then resolve the four viewpoints to reach an agreement as quickly as possible.

4 viewpoints – card 1	
You and three friends are the only ones in the classroom and you see the next day's science test, dropped on the floor next to the teachers table. What should you do?	
Viewpoint 1 Look at the test and don't tell anyone	Viewpoint 2 Leave it alone and don't tell anyone – they might think we've looked at it
Viewpoint 3 Tell the teacher and don't look	Viewpoint 4 One of the group looks and the rest don't

4 viewpoints – card 2	
You make a raft to sail free from your shipwrecked island but it can only hold three people safely. What should you do?	
Viewpoint 1 All stay together on the island	Viewpoint 2 Two sail and hopefully find help and rescue the other two
Viewpoint 3 Not much food and water left, so leave one on the island	Viewpoint 4 All go on the raft even though it might capsize

Figure 5.4 Four viewpoint cards.

Workshop Five: Four examples of problems set on the uninhabited island

These scenarios show how the problems children solve using their new-found talk skills can have whatever focus is required within the planned work for the class. For the first three problems, the focus is 'Materials and Their Properties' from the science National Curriculum (NC). The groups need to be able to resolve their differences and reach an agreement in order to apply their science knowledge and understanding to get enough food and water to ensure their survival on the island. The fourth problem links to a real news story and is a Personal, social and health education (PSHE) and citizenship dilemma.

Only polluted water left!

You are getting low on water. All that is left is a barrel of polluted water. However, in the water is salt, sand and pebbles

You can use all the resources given to you to try to get some water that will be suitable

for boiling for your drinking water

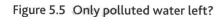

Figure 5.5 Only polluted water left?

Rice mix up!

You have a big separation problem – the rice we need to eat has been mixed up with peas, paper clips and sand

You can use all the resources given to you to try to separate these substances into piles of rice, peas, paper clips and sand

Figure 5.6 Rice mix up!

Freedom?

You have been on the island a while now, and though you have found some fruit, food and water supplies are starting to get very low. You decide that no-one is coming to rescue you so you decide to build a raft to escape the island. How will you build a raft? What are the best choices for materials?

However, when you make a raft to sail free from your shipwrecked island it can only hold three people safely. There are four of you. What should you do?

SOS

Figure 5.7 Freedom?

New discovery

A new island has been discovered in the Pacific Ocean. It has a rainforest, which scientists think may contain a new medicine, which will benefit many people.

However, the island is inhabited by a tribe of 25 people who have never seen anyone else. If the scientists visit, it puts them at risk from Western diseases and it could change their lifestyle forever.

What should be done?

Figure 5.8 New discovery.

Reflection

What is reflection and why is it important for effective talk?

In order for effective and lasting learning to take place, children need to be able to reflect on the quality of their talk in a range of contexts, both individually and as a group member, and then further develop their talk skills as a result of their reflection. However, we found that the children's ability to reflect on their talk was one of the hardest skills for them to develop. At a superficial level, children can easily answer questions that the teacher asks. However, no deep reflection and hence no effective learning will take place. Sinclair and Coulthard (1975) describe one typical

Photo 6.1 Reflection. How well did we use talk in our learning?

Reflection

type of teacher questioning as IRF – initiation, response, feedback – the most common form of teacher-child exchange, where the teacher asks the question, the child responds with the answer they think the teacher wants to hear, often a recall of facts, and the teacher feeds back with an acknowledgement of some kind. Thinking and learning are rarely extended in this type of exchange.

Early in the programme in the project schools, children began to tentatively develop a few thoughtful comments, such as one Year Five boy who said, 'I think I've reflected more, which has made me learn more', but even this does not really detail the link between the reflection and the child's developing learning. Often the children's reflections were very similar and were in a direct response to the questions they were asked to consider.

This chapter introduces a range of strategies that were used, with varying degrees of success, to help the children become more reflective.

Figure 6.1 shows what the children need to learn in order to be able to reflect on talk.

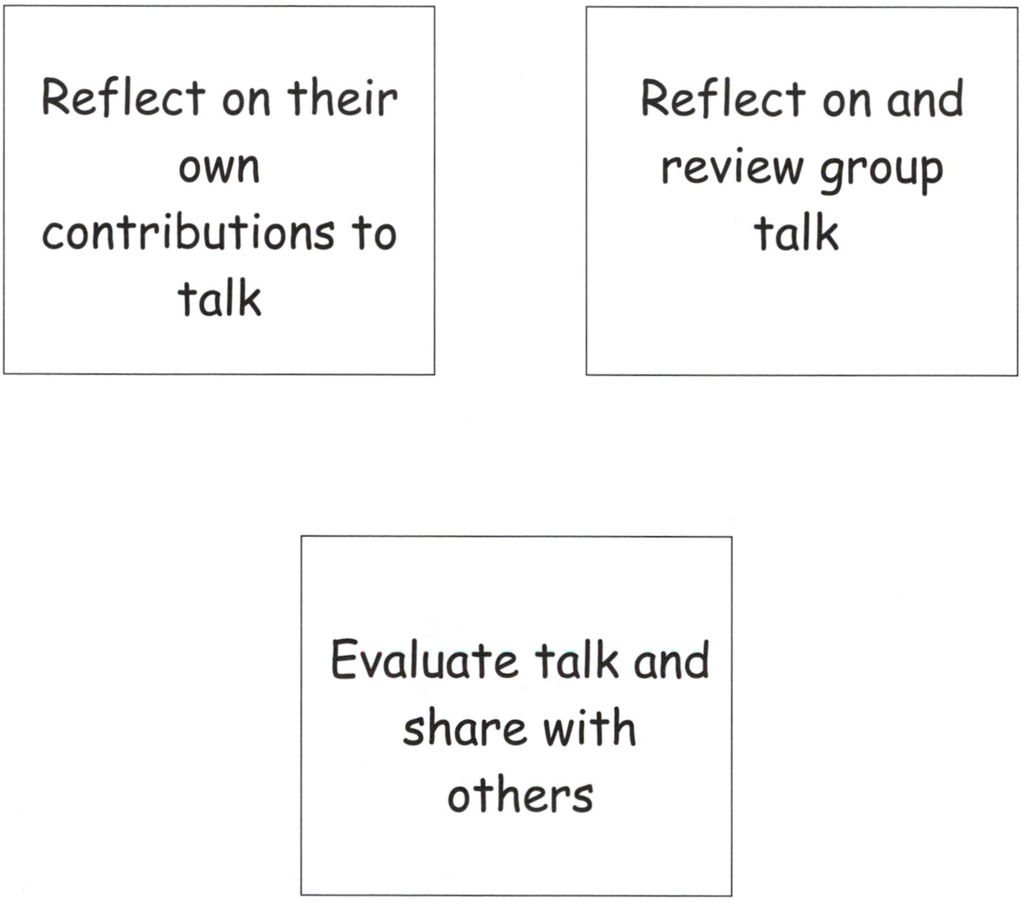

Reflect on their own contributions to talk	Reflect on and review group talk

Evaluate talk and share with others

Figure 6.1 What the children need to learn in order to be able to reflect.

Introduction to the reflection workshops:

The following workshops outline a range of activities that will help raise awareness of the importance of reflection and teach children how to use it to improve the quality of their talk:

- **Workshop One** is about collating phrases that help children to review and reflect on their talk. It provides prompt cards that can be used throughout the following activities.

- **Workshop Two** introduces the use of child observers to enable the children to review their group talk together.

- **Workshop Three** outlines how to apply the children's observation and reflection skills to evaluate adult and children's talk on video.

- **Workshop Four** outlines a range of methods that enable children to record their reflections.

- **Workshop Five** introduces the use of home learning talk tasks.

Workshop One: Prompt and phrase cards

In order for the children to be able to think of phrases that will help them to reflect, each group needs time reviewing video footage of their dialogues on a regular basis. The videos provide 'permanent evidence that can be revisited' (QCA, 1999: 11) but also provide extremely powerful ways of using AfL, through enabling both teacher and children's self and peer reflection to occur. After viewing one videoed group activity, a child in the project schools commented, 'I used to think I talked perfectly with people and that I listened well, but I wasn't as good as I thought'. Some of the children's perceptions of how their group talked were challenged by this evaluation process, and words like 'shocked', 'surprised' and 'amazed' were used in their subsequent dialogues. One child commented in the diary room that, 'we saw our first videos and we were shocked . . . well not really shocked but we didn't know we were that bad. We were shouting and not really saying anything much and we were being quite rude to each other.' The videos enabled children to understand the need to reflect both on their individual contributions and their personal responsibility for the quality of the talk and also their responsibility to the group. By watching videos of their talk at different stages of the programme, children were also empowered to reflect on their progress over time.

Figure 6.2 shows a set of prompt cards that were devised and used by the children.

Prompt cards:

Reflect

Think about how you have used talk and the learning dialogue in this task

Reflect

Discuss how the group have used talk and the learning dialogue in this task

Reflect

Discuss whether the talk extended the thinking and learning

Phrase cards:

How well did we use talk to work and learn from each other?

How well did I use my talk in this task?

What have I learnt that I can use next time?

What aspects of the learning dialogue do we need to work on?

Figure 6.2 Prompt and phrase cards.

Learning through Talk, Routledge © Heather Luxford and Lizzie Smart 2009

Workshop Two: Introducing observers

Children need to be taught to act as observers in their groups and to feedback on the quality of the talk that occurs. This is the only group role we advocate as we believe that children should not focus on their role in the group at the expense of the talk. We found that observers become empowered by their role in the debriefing process following talk sessions and all children appreciate getting feedback from a peer rather than from a teacher.

In order to carry out the observations it is helpful to have a checklist. The children should devise the checklists themselves, so that this activity is not only successful in providing ownership for the children but also in enabling them to reflect on what constitutes an effective learning dialogue. For example, following her observation of one group, a Year Five girl in one of the project schools commented that there was not enough back and forth responses between two children when they challenged each other. She explained, 'It is with this back and forth in our group that our ideas really take off.'

It is useful for the checklist to include visual and phrase prompts and, because the whole group will have worked on it together, the debriefing sessions following the talk activities will be easily understood by all concerned. The following are two examples of children's checklists devised in the project schools. The children colour coded their questions to match the six skills and added some cartoons after the sheets had been printed to help them 'read' them at speed.

Reflection

Dialogue Skill	Write what the group did well 😊	Write what the group need to work on ☹
How well did you participate?		
How well did you collaborate?		
How well did you build-on?		
How well did you challenge each other?		
How well did you resolve and reach agreement?		
How well did you reflect on your talk?		

	Dialogue Skill	Tally Chart – How many times do I answer yes to the question?
☹	Is anyone not joining in?	
☹	Has someone used a vague word such as 'thingy'?	
😊	Have they checked everyone understands what they're doing?	
😊	Has someone encouraged someone else to join in?	
😊	Has someone built-on to what's been said?	
😊	Has someone asked an open question?	
😊	Has someone asked, 'what does that mean?' and/or 'why do you think that?'	
😊	Have they given a summary of what's been said and asked if everyone agrees?	

Figure 6.3 Group observation grids.

Learning through Talk, Routledge © Heather Luxford and Lizzie Smart 2009

Photo 6.2 Group with an observer

Workshop Three: Evaluating video

The use of adult role-play videos has been discussed throughout the chapters in this book. At this stage, when the children in the project schools were confident to use all six of the talk skills, it proved useful for them to act as observers and evaluate these videos again. This enabled them to reflect on the talk being used and to set definite targets for each adult to work on. The children particularly enjoyed this role reversal but it also had benefits in enabling the children to become more skilled in setting their own realistic targets.

Children can also be shown excerpts of pupils talking from, for example, DfES videos to evaluate. There are advantages to using such videos, as they immediately ring true and enable the children to identify with the participants. Here they can see children like themselves, doing what they do. In the project schools, three extracts were used from the video of classroom examples that accompanies the pack 'Speaking, Listening, Learning' (DfES, 2003d). The first is of a group of Year Two pupils (screen reference 25.00–26.24) and the children soon spotted how not all children in the group were contributing. One girl commented, 'that boy is taking over the group; he's even whispering to the others what to say'. The second and third clips are of Year Four groups (screen references 39.55–41.20 and 49.04–50.58). The children's responses revealed how much they had learnt in the very mature, detailed dialogues that took place. For example, one group were impressed by the length of the contributions that were used, but were surprised because there was not much building on of ideas, noting, 'they might be giving detailed answers but they are still not talking as a group. They justify their own views and then just vote. I'd want to reach an agreement!' This not only highlighted the progress in the children's learning for the teacher but also very clearly for themselves.

Workshop Four: Talk logs and diary rooms

Talk logs

Talk logs are not new. As long ago as the latter half of the last century, the National Oracy Project recommended their use. The DfES also suggests 'systematically collecting tangible evidence of talk' and recommends 'written logs and diaries' as one means of doing so (DfES, 2003b). Logs enable children to record individual reflections but in the project schools we found they were initially problematic, as the children needed significant amounts of support to complete them, either because they were not sure what to write or because they struggled with technical aspects of writing and were inhibited because of this. There was a real irony in reflections on talk being recorded in writing, which was not lost on the children. For example, one Year Four boy explained, 'I didn't see much point in writing in it, because we knew what we had done and had already talked about how it had gone.' However, a Year Five girl disagreed, explaining, 'I thought it was good because each week you could look back and see what we had learnt.' As the programme progressed, children found it easier to make entries in their logs as they developed the meta-language to do so. However, it was always noticeable that the logs were less detailed than the responses received from the video diary room.

Video diary room

It is undoubtedly the case that the video diary room (stolen shamelessly from the *Big Brother* format) was the most successful method of reflection for the children in the project schools and provided the greatest insight into their learning for the teachers. Most children knew clearly how this idea worked from their viewing of the television programme and while the content material under discussion was certainly not on offer in the *Big Brother* house, the model of how to talk to the web-cam was!

This example of harnessing popular culture to good effect was more successful than we initially imagined. It was introduced as an alternative method of recording for those children who found the talk logs hard going. However, it soon became clear that it was more appropriate to record observations about talk using talk for all pupils and the length and quality of the reflections thus recorded was much better than any other method used. After the activities focused on building on, one child noted in his talk log that he found 'that building on is a really good life skill'. However, a much more developed and reflective response was recorded in the diary room when another child noted, 'I don't think build-on is useful all the time. Sometimes you just need to get it said quickly. However, when you've just had a long run of different ideas I think build-on would be useful'. This reflection showed real understanding of how and when to apply the skills, which was not obvious from any other source of reflection.

In the Diary Room the children were on their own, spoke at length to the camera, and as a teacher it was possible to gain many insights from what was said. For example, a Year Five boy, who was reflecting on his group, commented:

> It's Rick I am really concerned about because he's not getting involved in the talk, and that's my main problem because I don't know how to get him involved, and when I say it to anyone they say we are not letting him get a word in. But we do keep on saying Rick what do you think? But he just sits there going erm, well, erm, erm well . . .

Photo 6.3 Video diary room

At this stage in the research, Jim's comments in his talk log were short and bland and did not show the extent to which he was reflecting on his group's progress.

An example of a Year Five girl talking in the Diary Room is given in Video 11 on the website.

Workshop Five: Spreading the word: Talk and home learning

In order to involve other classes in the school and the family, it is possible at this stage to help the children to teach what they have learnt. Time needs to be spent in school devising ways to adapt what has been done to teach the dialogue skills at home. The use of the laminated prompt and phrases cards becomes useful here as the children develop teaching ideas. The following activities can be used to enhance home learning in two ways:

The first is for each child to introduce the six dialogue skills to someone at home. The children can produce posters, booklets and their own videos in school, which can then be copied and taken home to use as teaching resources with other family members to teach how to use talk for learning.

Second, talk tasks can be set as home learning tasks, which need to be completed by engaging in dialogue with other family members. These tasks can be linked to the class topic, or be general topics of the children's choosing. Back in school, each child can then summarise their family's view in class dialogues. If talk is the focus throughout the whole school, then the same talk task can be set for every class, so that whole families can discuss the topic at home, before all the children continue the dialogue in class or even assembly. These will need to be quite general topics for talk that will be appropriate across the age range. Figure 6.4 gives some examples.

Using Talk for Home Learning

What would your family bury in a time capsule to show what family life is like in the early 21st century?

Using Talk for Home Learning

How many words can you collect which you could use instead of talk.
For example: whisper, screech, gossip and chat

Using Talk for Home Learning

Your family has been given the opportunity to invite a famous person from now or the past to come to dinner. Who would it be and why?

Using Talk for Home Learning

Dr Who is about to return on the TV – if your family was in the next episode where would you take the TARDIS?

Figure 6.4 Home learning tasks.

Conclusion

Throughout this book, we hope we have given a flavour of how exciting it is to work with the children and observe their development in learning through talk. At first glance, some of the skills developed through the workshops might seem very straightforward but none was easy to achieve for the children, many of whom found this style of learning completely new. On watching some of the video examples on the website, it is noticeable that many groups started the programme convinced that they 'knew how to do it already' but can be seen almost coming to blows during relatively simple talk tasks. However, by the end of the programme, these same children were able to engage in detailed and sustained learning dialogues and were immensely proud of themselves as learners. Their meta-cognitive ability had rocketed and they knew it. As teachers, it was impossible not to share their pride and satisfaction. Whole class dialogues stopped being a ping-pong game of teacher/child utterances. Genuine questions were asked where all learners, teachers and TAs included, had a real interest in the answers. Learning improved dramatically and teaching became much more enjoyable as a result.

We are aware that we have included little about assessment as a discrete aspect of the teaching programme. This is deliberate and supports our view that assessment is integral. At every stage of the programme, teachers and children were engaged in formative assessment; AfL. They reflected on the learning and put these reflections to good use in the work that followed.

In 2003 the DfES noted, 'it is important to separate children's skills and achievement from the social dimensions of groups' (DfES, 2003b: 29). However, our belief is that it is these very 'social dimensions of groups' that enable the skills discussed in the previous chapters to develop. We believe that classrooms are social as well as academic centres and that learning is a social as well as an individual activity. As we have stated from the very first chapter, it is the ability to recognise and harness the social 'niceties' of group work, and to value and encourage every participant's contribution, that underpins effective learning dialogue. It therefore took a central place in all of our considerations.

The assessment of talk has also long been recognised as posing particular challenges for teachers. The QCA noted, 'talk does not leave permanent evidence which can be revisited' (QCA, 1999: 11). Talk can certainly be ephemeral but we believe it is possible to record evidence to revisit and that the nature of the evidence recorded can be very helpful in enabling both teachers and children to track progress in the development of the talk skills discussed in all the previous chapters. We think we have demonstrated that in the reflection chapter through the use of observers, talk logs, video diaries and the frequent use of video evaluations. The children found these assessment strategies purposeful and engaging. Shoulders did not droop at the word assessment in any of the classes involved in the project.

During the teaching programme, the children's ability to use the talk skills was also assessed and recorded regularly by the teacher on a group learning dialogue assessment sheet (see Resource 8.12). The DfES (2003b: 30) state that the length of contributions should not be assessed. While accepting that it is the quality of talk that matters, we found a direct correlation between length (especially the ability to build-on) and quality of contribution and for that reason, it is included in the group assessment sheet. This is a complex recording device and requires dedicated teacher time to use it effectively but it was very useful in the project school despite this. The fact that pupils became so much more confident in working independently enabled this recording to happen.

Perhaps the best endorsement of the programme comes from teachers and TAs who were not directly involved in it. A teacher working in one of the project schools commented that 'many more children are contributing to class discussions. The children know their contributions are encouraged and valued and have produced much better quality discussions'. Support for this view also came from other teachers, TAs, parents and the children themselves in both project schools.

A fitting closing word comes from a TA, who commented following her work with a group that included a child on the autistic spectrum, 'I can't believe how well they have just worked together. They used everything they'd already learnt and challenged each other in such a positive way. I didn't think Tim could do that.'

CHAPTER 8

Photocopiable resources

This section provides a range of resources that can be photocopied for use in the classroom.

(Resources 8.2 to 8.7 give a summary of each skill. These need to be photocopied onto different coloured card so each skill is colour coded. This really helps the children when using the cards in a group dialogue):

Resource 8.1: Summary of the six talk skills.

Resource 8.2: Participation – Summary of prompt and phrase cards.

Resource 8.3: Collaboration – Summary of prompt and phrase cards.

Resource 8.4: Build-On – Summary of prompt and phrase cards.

Resource 8.5: Positive Challenge – Summary of prompt and phrase cards.

Resource 8.6: Resolve and reach agreement- Summary of prompt and phrase cards.

Resource 8.7: Reflection – Summary of prompt and phrase cards.

Resource 8.8: Examples of emotion cartoon faces (Chapter One: Workshop One)

Resource 8.9: Talk Triangles Cards (Chapter Three: Workshop Three)

Resource 8.10: Set of Build-On cards (Chapter Three: Workshop Three)

Resource 8.11: Set of Character cards (Chapter Four: Workshop Three)

Resource 8.12: An example of a group learning dialogue assessment sheet.

Learning through Talk – Developing a Learning Dialogue

1. Participate
- Participation is about joining in and taking part. In order for each child to get the most from talking with others, they must all be emotionally secure enough to participate in the talk

Let's all…

2. Collaborate
- Collaboration involves working together and cooperating with each other. Each child has an individual and group responsibility for the talk and task in hand

What should we all be doing?

3. Build On
- Children need to learn how to build on their ideas and extend their talk. This will allow deeper learning to take place as they question and expand on their ideas and sustain the talk needed to extend their thinking and understanding

I agree/disagree because… What if..?

4. Positive Challenge
- Positive challenge includes being able to discuss different viewpoints and have these alternative viewpoints challenged by asking for clarification and justification. Challenging will extend each child's thinking

What do you mean by that? Why do you think that?

5. Resolve
- Dialogue is about resolving differences and reaching a common understanding. Children need to learn to sustain their talk to reach a consensus and agreement in order for deeper learning to take place

Do we all agree or shall we discuss it some more? So we have all agreed to…

6. Reflect
- Individuals and groups need to be able to reflect on their talk and evaluate how it improved their thinking and learning

How well did we use talk to work and learn from each other?

Resource 8.1 Summary of the skills.

1. Participation

The children need to be able to:

Be aware of their own emotions and of others around them	Understand the impact of these emotions on how confident we feel to participate	Understand we all need to contribute and share ideas

	Be able to stay on task

Children's Prompt Cards

Participation: Make sure everyone is on task	Participation: Put forward one of my ideas	Participation: Take part in the dialogue

Children's phrase cards

One of my ideas is…

What I think is…

Let's all…

Are we all concentrating?

Resource 8.2 1. Participation.

2. Collaboration

The children need to be able to:

Work together to clarify and plan what to do	Use active listening skills	Encourage others to participate to ensure everyone contributes	Respect others and respect that they may have a different viewpoint

Children's Prompt Cards

Collaboration:

Listen and try to understand what others are saying

Collaboration:

Make it clear what you have to do. Plan what to do to solve this problem

Collaboration:

Have your say, but don't let anyone dominate

Collaboration:

Make sure everyone in the group has spoken

Children's phrase cards

I wonder what ... thinks

Are we all clear what we have to do?

Have we all given an idea?

What should we all be doing?

Resource 8.3 2. Collaboration.

3. Building-On

The children need to be able to:

Add more detail to their own or others' ideas	Use questions to extend the Dialogue	Clarify their own or others' ideas
	Give feedback to previous contributions	Offer an alternative view or idea
		Give longer responses and sustain ideas over a sequence of responses

Children's Prompt Cards

Build and Extend:
Offer a different reason why

Build and Extend:
Make sure my ideas are clear and I don't use vague words

Build and Extend:
Give longer answers and have chains of dialogue

Build and Extend:
Respond and add to someone else's idea

I agree because…

What do you think?

I like that idea because…

Children's phrase cards

Resource 8.4 3. Building-on.

4. Positive Challenge

The children need to be able to:

Ask higher order questions	Ask for clarification	Ask for justification
		Challenge and reject viewpoints in a constructive way

Positive Challenge: Ask for a justification – ask why they think that	**Positive Challenge:** Ask for clarification – ask what they mean
Positive Challenge: Ask good open questions	**Positive Challenge:** Challenge other's ideas in a polite and respectful way

Why do you think that?

What do you mean by that?

What would happen if?

I'm not sure about that because...

Resource 8.5 4. Positive challenge.

Learning through Talk, Routledge © Heather Luxford and Lizzie Smart 2009

5. Resolve and reach agreement

The children need to be able to:

Generalise or summarise the ideas	Check for agreement	Bring task to a conclusion	Reach a Consensus and agreement

Children's Prompt Cards

Resolve: Give a summary of what's been said	Resolve: Propose a decision	Resolve: Check whether everyone agrees	Resolve: Give an answer or solution to the problem

Children's phrase cards

So what are we all saying?

What do we all agree on?

Do we all agree or shall we discuss it some more?

So we have all decided to…

Resource 8.6   5. Resolve and reach agreement.

6. Reflection

The children need to be able to :

Reflect on own contributions to talk	Review group talk	Evaluate talk and share with others

Children's Prompt Cards

Reflect:
Think about how you have used talk and the learning dialogue in this task

Reflect:
Discuss how the group have used talk and the learning dialogue in this task

Reflect:
Discuss whether the talk extended the thinking and learning

Children's phrase cards

How well did we use talk to work and learn from each other?

How well did I use my talk in this task?

What have I learnt that I can use next time?

What aspects of the learning dialogue do we need to work on?

Resource 8.7 6. Reflection.

Resource 8.8 Set of examples of emotion cartoon faces.

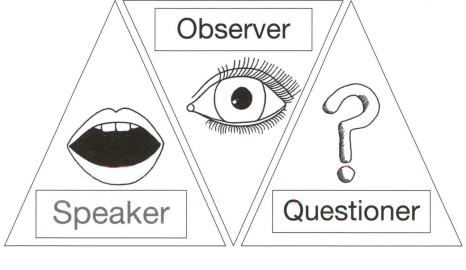

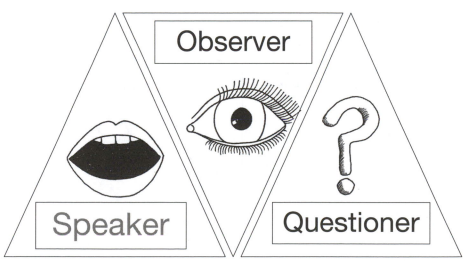

Resource 8.9 Set of Talk Triangle cards.

Resource 8.10 Set of build-on cards.

Learning through Talk, Routledge © Heather Luxford and Lizzie Smart 2009

Resource 8.11 Set of character cards.

Learning Dialogue – Using the main features of Learning Dialogue as an Assessment Tool			
Learning Task:	Date:	Total no. of contributions =	
The Group: Names 1)	2)	3)	4)

Keep a tally for each child …

Participate – Taking part.	Child no. 1	Child no. 2	Child no. 3	Child no. 4
Has contributed to dialogue	1)	2)	3)	4)

Collaborate – Working together.

	Child no. 1	Child no. 2	Child no. 3	Child no. 4
At start: Has clarified what to do – planned and organised task	1)	2)	3)	4)
During task: Has clarified what to do	1)	2)	3)	4)
Has tried to bring another back on task	1)	2)	3)	4)
Has responded to other viewpoints given	1)	2)	3)	4)
Has encouraged and supported contribution of others	1)	2)	3)	4)
Has ensured that everyone contributed	1)	2)	3)	4)

Build-on – Extend the dialogue.

	Child no. 1	Child no. 2	Child no. 3	Child no. 4
Has given feed-back to the previous contribution	1)	2)	3)	4)
Has added detail to the previous contribution	1)	2)	3)	4)
Used questions to extend dialogue	1)	2)	3)	4)
Has clarified own ideas	1)	2)	3)	4)
Proposed an alternative view or a new line of enquiry	1)	2)	3)	4)

Resource 8.12 Assessment sheet.